STEP-UP
HISTORY

The Great Famine

Feargal Brougham and Caroline Farrell

Evans

Published by Evans Brothers Limited
2A Portman Mansions
Chiltern Street
London W1U 6NR

© Evans Brothers Limited 2007

Produced for Evans Brothers Limited by
White-Thomson Publishing Ltd,
Bridgewater Business Centre,
210 High Street,
Lewes, East Sussex BN7 2NH

Printed in China

Project manager: Sonya Newland

Designer: Robert Walster

Consultant: Brian Malone

British Library Cataloguing in Publication Data

Brougham, Feargal

The Great Famine. - (Step up Ireland)
1. Ireland - History - Famine, 1845-1852 -
Juvenile literature

I. Title II. Farrell, Caroline
941.5'081

ISBN-13: 9780237533915

Picture acknowledgements:

Corbis: pages 14 and cover, top right (David J.
& Janice L. Frent Collection), 15 (Robert Wallis),
18, 21b (Michael St. Maur Sheil), 23, 26 and
cover top left (Michael St. Maur Sheil), 27 (Richard
Cummins); Getty Images: page 25 (Hulton
Archive); Courtesy of the National Library of
Ireland: pages 4, 9, 10l, 10r, 21t, 22, 24; Jon
Swallow: 11, 12 and cover; Topfoto.co.uk: pages
1 (Fotomas), 7 (Topham Picturepoint), 8 (HIP), 13
(Topham Picturepoint), 16 (Fotomas), 17 (Fotomas),
19, 20 (Fotomas).

Illustrative work by Robert Walster.

Contents

What was the Great Famine?

Between the years 1845 and 1851, a terrible famine took place in Ireland. One million people died of starvation and disease, and another million left Ireland, never to return. These people died and emigrated because of the repeated failure of the potato crop, the staple diet of the Irish poor.

Ireland and Britain

Ireland had been controlled by Britain for nearly seven centuries when the Famine took place. Since the Act of Union in 1801, Ireland had been part of the United Kingdom, and all laws for Ireland and the Irish people were made by the parliament in London.

Most of the land in Ireland was divided into huge estates. These estates were owned by landlords, who often lived far away in England and rarely came to Ireland at all. The Irish people were farmers and tenants who lived on the land. They had to pay high rents, so they grew food and raised livestock to pay those rents.

◀ A poor family in Ireland gathers round a pile of potatoes that have been ruined by a disease called blight. The failure of the potato crop was the biggest cause of the Great Famine because potatoes were the main source of food for most people.

About this book

In this book you will find out what happened during the six years of the Great Famine in Ireland. What caused it? What was life like for the poor people in Ireland? How did they get help and what happened after the Famine was over?

Because the Famine happened around 160 years ago, there is lots of information about it from many different sources. Some of this information comes from books, newspaper articles, government reports and letters. There are also many eyewitness accounts from ordinary people who lived in Ireland, as well as people who travelled through the country at the time and reported what they had seen. You can read some of these accounts in this book.

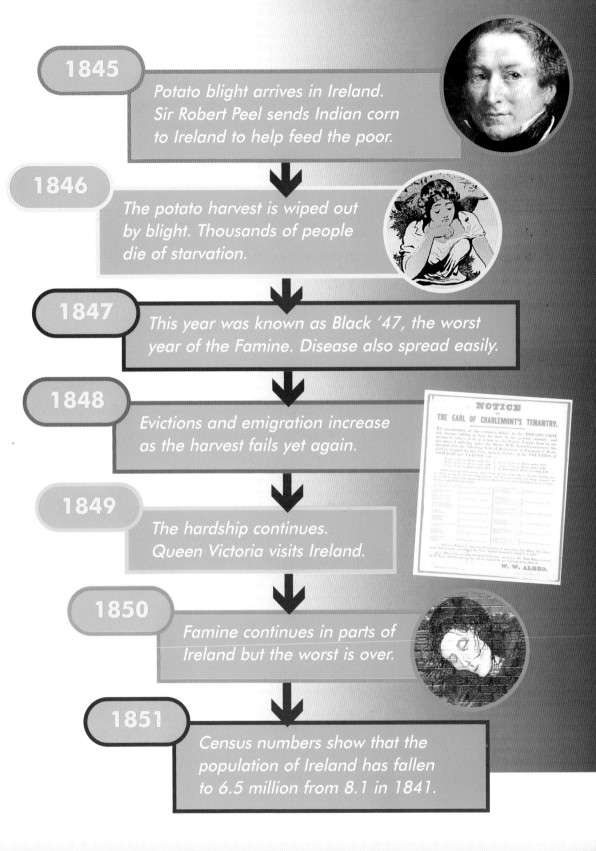

1845 Potato blight arrives in Ireland. Sir Robert Peel sends Indian corn to Ireland to help feed the poor.

1846 The potato harvest is wiped out by blight. Thousands of people die of starvation.

1847 This year was known as Black '47, the worst year of the Famine. Disease also spread easily.

1848 Evictions and emigration increase as the harvest fails yet again.

1849 The hardship continues. Queen Victoria visits Ireland.

1850 Famine continues in parts of Ireland but the worst is over.

1851 Census numbers show that the population of Ireland has fallen to 6.5 million from 8.1 in 1841.

Ireland before the Famine

The reasons why the Famine had such a devastating effect have their roots in events that took place in Ireland centuries before the Famine occurred. For hundreds of years, the rulers of England had wanted to control their neighbouring island of Ireland. During the sixteenth century, when Elizabeth I was queen, many Protestant English and Scottish settlers were given land in Ireland. The native Irish people, most of whom were Catholics, were cleared from their homes and farms, often by force, to make way for the new settlers. This was known as the time of Plantations.

The new settlers distrusted the Irish, and in turn the Irish were hostile to the newcomers. There were many rebellions and wars between the two groups.

▶ *Ireland is divided into four provinces – Ulster, Leinster, Munster and Connaught. When Cromwell's soldiers invaded Ireland, many people fled to the westernmost province of Connaught for safety.*

'To Hell or to Connaught'

In 1649, Oliver Cromwell, the Lord Protector of England, decided to put an end to the Irish rebellions once and for all. He went to Ireland with a large force of soldiers – anyone who resisted was threatened and their lands were confiscated. Those who would not give in and support the English parliament were told by Cromwell to go 'to Hell or to Connaught'. Connaught was a province in the far west of Ireland, with the poorest land.

▶ During the invasion of Ireland, Oliver Cromwell's soldiers seized the town of Drogheda in eastern Ireland and massacred its inhabitants. Nearly 3,000 Irish people died.

Penal Laws

By the time of the Great Famine, very few Irish people actually owned the land they farmed. This was because of the Penal Laws, introduced by the British parliament in 1695. They said:

- No Catholic could buy or inherit land from Protestants

- Catholics were not allowed to vote or become members of parliament

- Catholic children were not allowed to go to school unless they became Protestant

When the Penal Laws were finally repealed, over 95 per cent of land in Ireland was owned by Protestants of English and Scottish descent. Irish people had little education and were often very poor.

Act of Union

In 1801, the United Kingdom of Great Britain and Ireland was formed. From this time on, all decisions about Ireland were made by parliament in London, by men who had little knowledge of or connection to the country.

Precious potatoes

Some historians have suggested that the reason potatoes became such an important food was because they were easy to store below the soil. Hidden like this, they would not be destroyed like grain, even if Cromwell's soldiers burned the fields.

Potato blight

In the autumn of 1845, disaster struck Ireland. Potato blight arrived. Blight is a type of fungus that destroys potatoes. Its seeds are carried through the air and spread easily in the damp Irish climate. These seeds infect the potato plant, causing it to develop black spots. The leaves wither and the stalks turn black. Even the potato underground is affected – it turns into a soggy, black mass. A horrible smell fills the air near potato fields affected by blight.

When the farmers harvested their precious potatoes in 1845, they found them rotten and inedible. It is thought that in 1845 nearly half of the country's potato harvest was affected by this disease. Blight, like the potato itself, probably originated in America and spread to mainland Europe, Britain and Ireland on ships' cargoes.

▶ *This page from a French encyclopedia shows all the diseases that can affect potato crops. In the middle is blight (Phytophtera infestans), the disease that destroyed the harvest in Ireland in 1845, starting the Great Famine.*

The blight in Ireland

Blight also affected potato crops in other parts of Europe, but it did not cause the same human catastrophe as it did in Ireland. The people could not turn to other foods like grain and vegetables. Irish farmers were very poor – almost three million people ate potatoes for

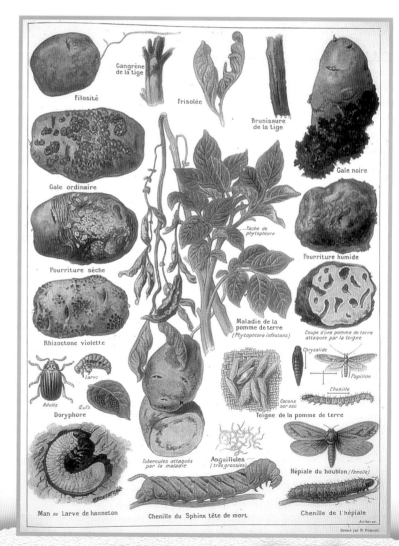

breakfast, lunch and dinner. Some men might eat up to 60 small potatoes a day! They could be boiled or mashed with buttermilk or included in stews. Any leftovers could be made into potato cakes. The potato is very nutritious as it is packed with vitamins and minerals. If people drank some buttermilk with their potatoes they were almost getting a balanced diet.

Lazy beds

Potatoes were grown in raised beds known as 'lazy beds'. These were created by laying manure and seaweed in rows about a metre apart as fertiliser. Then furrows were dug and the soil from them was piled on top of the fertiliser. The seed potatoes were planted in the middle of this raised bed. The Lumper, or Horse Potato, variety was one of the most popular types of potato used by the Irish poor, as it grew well even in poor soil. Unfortunately, it was also particularly prone to diseases like blight.

Where did potatoes come from?

Using websites such as http://indepthinfo.com/potato/ and http://www.factmonster.com find out more about where the potato came from. Where were potatoes first grown? How and when did they come to Britain and Ireland?

◄ Planting and harvesting potatoes was hard work. The fields would be dug by spade, and planting and fertilising were done by hand. It was important work, though. One acre of potato field could support a family of four, whereas an acre of grain could only support two people.

The land system

By the time of the Great Famine, land in Ireland was under the control of about 22,000 landowners, or landlords. They were often away from their estates for long periods of time. The landlord earned money from the rent he charged tenants. Some landlords just wanted as much money as possible from their tenants, but others were kind men who tried to help the people who lived on their land during the six long years of the Famine.

Agents

Agents managed the estates for the landlords. They were responsible for setting the price of the rent each year, and for collecting it. Dishonest agents often charged higher rents to make extra money for themselves.

Large farmers

Large farmers rented land on a long lease from the landlord. In order to pay their rent, they sub-let land to smaller farmers. They owned good houses with four or five rooms. They and their families ate potatoes, oats, eggs and bacon, and their children went to school.

▲ Wealthy landlords like these were at the top of the land system. Many of them were known as 'absentee landlords', because they spent long periods away from their land.

▲ Large farmers might have between 10 and 1,000 acres of land. Their houses were quite large compared to cottiers' cottages.

Small farmers

Small farmers rented about five acres of land. They grew oats and potatoes, and kept a pig and a few chickens. They survived on their crop of potatoes. Tenant farmers divided their land between their sons when they married. This made farm sizes smaller and smaller.

▲ *Small farmers lived in thatched cottages like this, usually with just one room.*

Cottiers

Cottiers worked for the large farmers and were among the poorest people. They lived in a one-roomed cabin, which had no windows and just a hole in the roof to let out the smoke from the fire. They grew enough potatoes to supply their family for a year. They earned no money, but just worked to pay the rent.

Labourers

Labourers were called spalpeens. They travelled around, taking work where they could find it. They would rent a piece of ready-dug and ready-manured land from the farmer, known as Conacre. They could plant a few potatoes here and then go and work elsewhere, returning later for the harvest. They lived in makeshift cabins. A labourer's family depended entirely on the potato harvest to survive.

Life on the land

Imagine you belonged to one group from the Irish land pyramid. Using the information in this book and other resources, write a diary entry about a day in your life. Think about what you would have to eat and what your living conditions would be like. Include some information about the other people in the land system and your family's relationship to them.

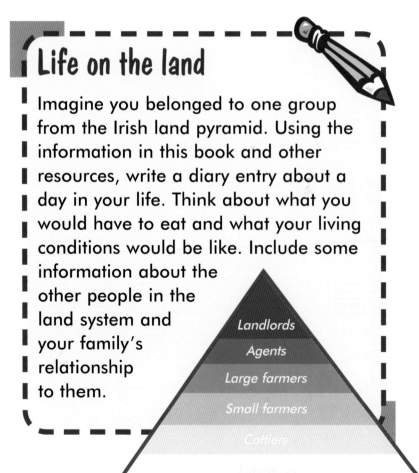

Peel's Brimstone

Sir Robert Peel was the prime minister of Britain in 1845, at the start of the Great Famine in Ireland. People at that time believed that governments should not interfere in the economy of a country and should not give out free food. This idea was known as laissez-faire, which means 'let things take their own course'.

Robert Peel believed in this idea, but he also knew that people in Ireland would die of starvation if he did nothing. So in 1845, he secretly bought £100,000 worth of Indian corn (sweetcorn) and arranged for it to be shipped to Ireland from America. It was sold cheaply to families whose potato crops had failed.

Corn porridge

Most people in Ireland had never seen corn before and they did not know how to cook it properly. They ground it up to make a type of yellow, gritty porridge, or stirabout. Often this was not cooked for long enough and made people sick. It became known as 'Peel's Brimstone'.

Although Peel's efforts certainly helped many, some of the poorest people had no money at all to buy the corn. It was also difficult to transport it to the most remote areas, like the west of Ireland, because the roads were so bad.

▶ *The Irish poor only had basic cooking facilities in their cottages. They would boil up the corn in a pot or kettle over the fireplace to make a type of porridge.*

The Relief Commission

Peel ordered that a Relief Commission be started to organise food aid for Ireland. The Commission had to find food depots where the corn could be stored. It also set up committees to organise the sale of the corn and to begin relief works. The committees were made up of local landlords or their agents and other important people in an area. Money was collected from people who were better off to help the poor. Half of the cost was paid by the government.

The government thought that relief works – or public works – would give people paid work. With the money they earned they could buy food. However, the people were so hungry that they were often too weak to work. Public works meant hard labour building roads or piers, or building systems to drain land.

▶ *The prime minister, Sir Robert Peel, took the first steps towards helping the Irish people in the first year of the Famine. He had to work secretly, as many people in the government did not think that England should get involved.*

Robert Peel's CV

Robert Peel acted out of a sense of what he thought was right, despite the government policies at the time. He had previous experience in Ireland and this gave him some ideas of how he might help the Irish people. Use the Internet and other resources to find out more about Robert Peel and write a CV for him. Include his personal details, and the key events that happened during his time as prime minister.

1846 – The crop fails again

Many Irish farmers believed that the blight would only affect their crops for one year. The potato harvest had failed before. Most people then had survived by eating any good parts of the diseased potatoes and selling their possessions to buy food.

In the spring of 1846, seed potatoes were planted with high hopes for the harvest. Chickens, pigs and furniture were sold to make it through until the autumn.

Disaster strikes

The harvest of 1846 was a total failure. Thousands of people, who were already nearly starving, succumbed easily to disease.

The eyewitness account below was written by a land agent, William S. Trench, in Co. Laois.

'On August 6, 1846 – I shall not readily forget the day – I rode up as usual to my mountain property, and my feelings may be imagined when before I saw the crop, I smelt the fearful stench, now so well known and recognised as the death sign of each field of potatoes…'

It was the same all over the country. Another eyewitness, Father Theobald Mathew, who worked in Cork, wrote this account in a letter dated 7 August 1846:

'On the 27th of last month I passed from Cork to Dublin, and this doomed plant bloomed in all the luxuriance of an abundant harvest. Returning on the 3rd, I beheld with sorrow one wide waste of putrefying vegetation. In many places the wretched people were seated on the fences of their decaying gardens, wringing their hands and wailing bitterly the destruction that had left them foodless.'

▲ Father Theobald Mathew was an Irish missionary. As he travelled around Ireland he was shocked by the effect the Famine was having on the poor.

Change in parliament

In June 1846, an election was held. Lord John Russell was chosen to be prime minister instead of Robert Peel. Lord Russell made two important changes to the help that Robert Peel had put in place. He stopped any more shipments of Indian corn going to Ireland. He also decided that half the cost of the relief works would no longer be provided by the government. The Irish landlords would have to bear all the cost themselves. The Irish people were devastated when they heard this news.

▶ *More than 150 years after the Famine, some people still blame the English for the suffering that occurred. This mural in Belfast uses the Famine to persuade people that the whole of Ireland should be independent from Britain. The words at the top, 'An Gorta Mór', are Irish for 'The Great Hunger'.*

Write a letter

Write a letter from Father Mathew to Lord John Russell explaining what you have seen on your journey from Dublin to Cork. Ask him to persuade the parliament to do more for Ireland. Give him as many practical suggestions as you can think of.

AN GORTA MÓR

BRITAIN'S GENOCIDE BY STARVATION

IRELAND'S HOLOCAUST 1845 1849

OVER 1,500,000 DEATHS

The workhouse

In Ireland in the nineteenth century, people who had no money could go to the workhouse. By the time of the Great Famine, there were around 130 workhouses in Ireland. These were designed to cope with a standard number of poor people in a district. When the Famine occurred, many more people than normal were forced to go there, and they became very overcrowded. By the spring of 1847, 116,000 destitute people were living in workhouses.

Once members of a family went into the workhouse they had to give up all rights to their land to prove that they really were destitute. The father was not allowed to remain behind to tend the land while his wife and children lived in the workhouse.

Life in the workhouse

In the workhouse, families were put into different parts of the complex. Men, women, boys and girls were all housed separately. Families were not allowed to remain together. They washed and gave up their clothes – they had to wear uniforms.

There were strict rules of behaviour. For example, talking during mealtimes was forbidden. People were set to work. The men had to break up stones that would be used for building and the women worked in the laundry or knitted. Children were given some basic schooling each day. Families never saw each other except perhaps at church on Sundays.

▶ *During the Famine, around 63,000 children were forced to live in workhouses. Many of them were orphans who had lost their parents to starvation or disease.*

Mealtimes

Meals were served twice a day. Before the Famine they consisted of oatmeal, potatoes and buttermilk. Once the Famine was at its height, however, the food served was often simply poor-quality oatmeal. Despite this, thousands of hungry people clamoured at the gates, begging for food or to be allowed to live in the workhouses.

Fever

Many people were so weakened by hunger that they caught diseases very easily. Famine fever was common and spread quickly in the overcrowded conditions of the workhouses. In the town of Kilrush, 99 people out of 101 in the workhouse's hospital wing died in one week alone.

▶ *Despite the harsh and unpleasant conditions in the workhouses, at the height of the Famine thousands of people flocked to them, begging to be allowed in.*

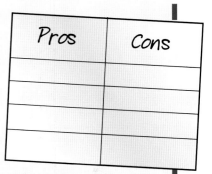

Pros and cons

Your family has no food and no money. You are trying to decide whether or not to go into the workhouse. Draw up a chart with two columns and write a list of advantages and disadvantages to help you make your decision. You can find more information about what life was like in the workhouse and why people went there at: http://www.workhouses.org.uk

Pros	Cons

Eviction

As the Famine grew worse, tenant farmers had no way to pay the rent to their landlords. Many landlords also faced financial difficulties. The government in London had passed an Act of Parliament that made landlords responsible for the poor on their land. This meant that the landlord had to pay extra taxes to help keep the workhouses open and feed the people. To avoid this expense, landlords started clearing their lands of unwanted tenants. Some paid for their tenants to emigrate while others simply removed or evicted the tenant farmer and his family.

An eviction

An eviction scene could see bailiffs, helped by soldiers or local militia, evict a family by force. The roof of the house would be removed to prevent the family returning. Then the walls might be tumbled down.

The choices facing the tenants after they were evicted were stark. They could try to enter the workhouse, emigrate or travel the country begging. A famous Quaker, James Hack Tuke, who worked and travelled in Ireland during the Famine, reported on an evicted family on a visit to Achill Island, Co. Mayo in 1847.

'One old grey-headed man came tottering up to us bearing in his arms his bedridden wife and, putting her down at our feet, pointed in silent agony to her, and then to his roofless dwelling, the charred timbers of which were scattered in all directions around.'

◀ Evicted families would often use the remains of their cabin to build a rough shelter in a ditch or at the side of the road. This was called a scalpeen.

Good and bad landlords

One landlord, Lord Lucan, evicted 2,000 people from his lands near Ballinrobe, Co. Mayo. Not all landlords resorted to eviction, though. George Henry Moore did his best to help the tenants on his estate. He gave a dairy cow to every widow on his land.

Historians know that between 1849 and 1854, nearly 50,000 families (a quarter of a million people) were evicted in Ireland. The counties that were worst affected were Clare, Mayo, and other parts of Connaught and Munster.

Famine report

Evictions took place all over Ireland in 1847. Create the front page of a newspaper that contains an article about an eviction you have just witnessed. Include a quote from the tenant farmer and the landlord – why has the landlord done this, and how does the tenant feel? Use the Internet to find a suitable photograph and include it with your article.

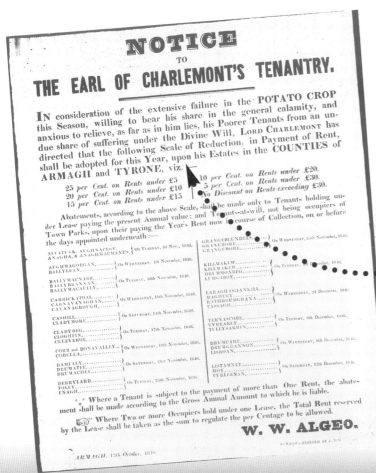

'In consideration of the extensive failure in the potato crop this Season, willing to bear his share in the general calamity, and anxious to relieve, as far as in him lies, his Poorer Tenants from an undue share of suffering under the Divine Will, Lord Charlemont has directed that the following Scale of Reduction, in Payment of Rent, shall be adopted for this Year...'

Not all landlords were cruel. Some tried to help their tenants. This is a notice to the Earl of Charlemont's tenants, telling them that he would reduce their rent.

Black '47

Even today the words Black '47 are still used in Ireland to describe the year 1847. This was the year that the Great Famine was at its height.

Different diseases

Typhus was also known as 'Famine fever'. It spread rapidly through lice in the dirty conditions of workhouses and people's homes. Dysentery was caught by drinking dirty water or water that had not been boiled properly. Typhus and cholera were contagious, so sometimes people who were trying to help the poor died themselves. In 1847, 40 Protestant clergymen died of Famine illnesses. Even though they were not hungry, they caught the fever from the people in their parishes.

Soup kitchens

The Society of Friends (also known as the Quakers) was a Christian group. Quakers believed it was their duty to help the poor. When the Famine began, they set up soup kitchens. These were centres where the poor could come and get a bowl of nourishing food. The Quakers risked their own lives working closely with people who had diseases.

Simple soup

Using the Internet and other resources, create a nourishing recipe for soup for you and your family. Try to include ingredients that are good for you, but remember not to spend too much. You can get some ideas for what ingredients you will need and how to prepare the soup on the following website: http://www.indepthinfo.com/potato/recipes.shtml

◀ *In early 1847, the government decided to set up its own soup kitchens. Nearly three million people were fed there every day.*

This picture comes from an Irish newspaper, the Weekly Freeman, *dating from 1880. It shows Ireland (the woman) mourning the loss of all the people who had died because of the Famine. She holds a piece of paper showing how the population of the country has decreased.*

Famine facts

- Almost a quarter of a million people died (249,335). There was little blight in 1847 but people still had no potatoes to eat. There had been few seed potatoes to plant.

- Disease was the biggest killer in Black '47. More people died from disease than from hunger.

- To make matters even worse, the winter of 1847 was a very cold one. There were so many storms that any fishermen who still had not sold their nets or boats in order to buy food could not go to sea to fish.

▼ *These ruins are all that is left of a village on Achill Island. Its inhabitants all died or left the village during the Great Famine.*

Famine stories

Throughout the years of the Famine many tragic events took place in Ireland. One of these happened in the remote area of Louisburgh, Co. Mayo. In the spring of 1849, a crowd of starving people gathered in the town, looking for help. They were told they needed to speak to the guardians of the workhouse.

The guardians were staying in Delphi, a fishing lodge around 16 kilometres away. To reach Delphi, the crowd had to walk over bogs, cross rivers, climb through a mountain pass and around a deep mountain lake. When the people reached Delphi, the guardians were at lunch and refused to help them. The people had no choice but to start the long return journey. On their way, the weather worsened and at least 12 people died from hunger and exhaustion. This journey is still remembered today by an annual Famine Walk along the route of the march to Delphi.

A visit from the queen

Queen Victoria was concerned about the reports she had received of famine in Ireland. She donated £2,000 to help relieve the suffering. In 1849, she paid her first visit to Ireland. Travelling on her royal yacht, the *Victoria and Albert*, she visited Cork, Kildare and Dublin, and noticed how poor and thin many people were. The Irish nicknamed her 'The Famine Queen'. Can you find out why?

▼ *The arrival of Queen Victoria on her royal yacht, on her first visit to Ireland in 1849.*

The Choctaw tribe

At the height of the Famine in 1847, an act of charity took place from an unlikely source. The Choctaw tribe of Native Americans donated $170 to the victims of the Irish Famine. This was a large amount of money in those days. The Choctaw were especially touched by the misery of the Irish people since they had also suffered terribly 15 years earlier. They had been forced to march 800 kilometres to new lands. Thousands had died along the way.

Cheshire schoolchildren

Many ordinary people in Britain collected money to help the victims of Famine in Ireland. In Cheshire, a group of schoolgirls also helped. They had read reports of the Famine, so they sent a small donation instead of having their yearly treat.

'Rev. Sir – We, the children belonging to the Moulton National School, in the parish of Davenharm (Cheshire), having heard from our beloved patroness, Mrs. Harper, of the distress that is so prevalent in our sister island, have given up our annual treat to the relief of our suffering sisters in Ireland... We humbly trust that our offering (small as it may appear), will be accepted.'

Emergency aid

What practical help can we give poor people in the world today? Use the Internet and other resources to find out what parts of the world are suffering famine today and why. How are other countries helping?

▲ *The plight of the Famine children encouraged people from other countries to send money to help them.*

Emigration and the 'Coffin Ships'

As the Great Famine continued, people realised they would die if they stayed on their land. There were few other choices. Some decided to risk everything, sell their last few possessions and emigrate. This meant leaving everything behind, usually for ever – their land, their friends and relatives – to go to seek their fortunes in a new country.

Liverpool

The port of Liverpool became the most popular place to go for many of the poorest Irish emigrants. It was a short voyage and not expensive. Once in Liverpool, the new arrivals lived in overcrowded slums, where disease spread quickly. Soon some of the people of Liverpool fell ill and died. The city council tried to send the emigrants back to Ireland and stop any more new arrivals. The Irish started travelling to other ports, like Glasgow, Bristol and London.

The New World

Where else could the Irish go to flee hunger and death? Australia was too expensive and too far away. Some landlords decided to pay for their tenants to go to America instead. It was cheaper to pay for the tenant to go away than to continue supporting them.

Soon the cities of Boston and New York in the United States and Quebec in Canada became the new destinations. It was not easy to get into the United States, though. Ships' captains had to pay a lot of money if they brought sick passengers into Boston or New York. Many ships sailed to Canada instead, where the rules were less harsh.

◀ *A poor man, with all his worldly possessions, looks at a poster for an emigration ship in Dublin harbour. This ship is sailing to New York – one of the most popular destinations for Irish emigrants.*

The Coffin Ships

During the Famine nearly 200,000 people emigrated each year. Some ships that carried people had originally been cargo ships. These had extra bunks installed and began transporting people instead. Life on board was very difficult. Captains were supposed to supply food and water, but the food that was provided was often of very poor quality. Because so many people died on the journey, these ships were nicknamed 'Coffin Ships'.

Conditions were very poor on board the Coffin Ships. There was often nowhere to wash and no toilets. Diseases spread quickly, and many people never reached the New World.

Emigration poster

Design a poster advertising the sailing of an emigrant ship. Remember to include the name of the ship, its destination, when it is leaving and from which port. See if you can find a picture of a Coffin Ship to include on the poster.

Legacy of the Famine

Blight struck the potato harvest in 1848 and again in 1849. People continued to die in large numbers from hunger and diseases. Evictions and emigration were common. By 1851, however, the worst was over. The six years of the Great Famine caused many changes to life in Ireland.

Population

The population of Ireland in the 1841 census was 8.1 million people. When the census was taken 10 years later, the population had fallen to 6.5 million. The counties with the biggest drops in population were Roscommon, Mayo, Sligo, Galway and Leitrim. Because so many people continued to emigrate, the population of Ireland kept falling for another 100 years.

Farm size

After the Famine, farms were bigger than before. Many of those who had died or emigrated were cottiers who had lived on very small farms. Their lands were put together to create larger farms. The practice of dividing a farm between all of a farmer's sons ended. The eldest son now inherited all the land.

▶ *This wall mural in Belfast shows women trying to grow potatoes during the Famine. Afterwards, survivors realised that they could not depend upon the potato alone to feed themselves. They would have to earn money to buy other foods.*

Politics

After the Famine, many Irish people felt that the Act of Union between Great Britain and Ireland was not working. Demands for Home Rule in Ireland increased.

Language

The number of people speaking the Irish language (*Gaeilge*) dropped by more than one million after the Famine. Many of the people who were Irish-language speakers lived in the counties that were worst affected. In the years that followed, people preferred their children to speak English because it would be more useful to them if they had to emigrate.

Emigration

Although Irish people emigrated to Britain and America before 1845, the Famine made emigration a normal part of life in Ireland. Today 40 million American citizens and about 10 million British people come from Irish families.

▶ *The Irish people still look back on the Great Famine as one of the worst events in the country's history. There are many memorials all over Ireland. This statue of Famine victims is in Dublin.*

An emigrant's letter

It is 20 years after the Famine. You are living in America. Tell your own son or daughter about what your life was like in Ireland during those years and why you left. Don't forget to explain how you travelled to America.

Glossary

abundant — plentiful.

Act of Union — the law that brought Ireland under the direct rule of the British parliament in London.

annual — happening every year.

bailiffs — landlord's agents who helped in evicting tenants.

beheld — noticed or observed.

buttermilk — the liquid that is left behind after milk has been churned and made into butter.

cargoes — goods carried aboard ships, for example, grain.

catastrophe — a terrible disaster.

Catholic — someone who follows a form of Christianity that believes in the traditions and teachings of the Roman Catholic Church and the authority of the Pope, as well as the Bible.

census — an official count of all the people living in a country.

clamoured — loudly demanded.

clergymen — priests or pastors who are leaders in a Christian religion.

confiscated — taken away by someone in authority, sometimes by force.

contagious — catching – for example a disease is contagious if it can be passed between people by contact.

depots — storehouses.

descent — a particular family background.

destitute — having nothing at all – no money and few possessions.

dwelling — home.

emigrate — to move to another country.

fertiliser — a substance such as manure that is added to the soil to make plants grow better.

fungus — an organism like a toadstool or mushroom that produces special seeds called spores.

furrows — long grooves dug into a field for planting crops.

guardians — the people in charge of a workhouse.

Home Rule — a proposed form of independence for Ireland, in which it would have its own parliament to rule on Irish issues.

hostile — unfriendly.

inedible — not fit to be eaten.

laissez-faire — the policy of non-interference in the economy of a country that was popular in the nineteenth century.

landlords	the owners of estates who rented land out to farmers.
lease	the contract or agreement between a landlord and tenant.
livestock	farm animals, for example pigs, cattle or chickens.
luxuriance	lush growth.
Lord Protector	the title given to Oliver Cromwell when he was ruling Britain in place of a king or queen.
manure	animal dung used to improve soil to help crops grow.
militia	a force of men taken from the general population – not belonging to an army but acting like one.
Native Americans	the people who lived in America before European settlers arrived.
nourishing	good for you.
nutritious	healthy and good for you.
originated	came from – origins are the place where something first happens, such as where the blight first appeared.
parliament	the place where elected representatives of the people make decisions and laws for a country.
Plantations	the handing over of land in Ireland to English and Scottish settlers.

Protestant	someone who follows a form of Christianity that rejects the teachings of the Roman Catholic Church and believes in the Bible as the only authority for Christians.
Quaker	a member of the Society of Friends.
relief works	government projects organised to allow poor people to earn money.
repealed	got rid of or abolished a law.
scalpeen	a shelter built at the side of the road or in a ditch, usually after an eviction.
slums	poor areas in a city, where housing is cheap and of low quality.
sources	documents or people from history that give us information and evidence about events in the past.
spalpeen	a wandering labourer. It is the English spelling of the Irish word *Spailpín*.
staple	a basic and most important item of food.
starvation	not having enough food to keep you alive.
stirabout	porridge.
sub-let	when a farmer leases out some land he is renting to another farmer.
succumbed	gave in to.
tenants	the people who rented land from landlords.

For teachers and parents

This book is designed to help children develop their knowledge, understanding and skills in Social, Environmental and Scientific Education. It is specifically focused on the strand 'Eras of Change and Conflict' within the Irish History curriculum.

Eyewitness accounts and other documentary evidence are included to assist children in considering and analysing their importance to the study of the topic. Furthermore, this evidence gives opportunities for children to view these events from the perspective of others and thus develop empathy and awareness. It also focuses on other skills involved in working as an historian. The chronological aspects of the Great Famine are stressed, as is the idea of cause and effect.

There had been a tendency in the past to view the causes of the Famine simplistically. Children are encouraged here to consider the many events that led to the Great Famine. Since this is a tragic and emotive period in Irish history it is important to present a balanced view. Reference is made in this book to events dealing with land ownership, social structure and colonisation prior to the Famine in order to deepen children's understanding of the events that followed.

The activities included throughout the book provide further opportunities for children to develop their understanding of the period and promote research using other sources, such as ICT. The activities are also designed with a view to integrating other curricular areas into children's study of the Famine, for example using art and geography where appropriate.

SUGGESTED FURTHER ACTIVITIES

Pages 4–5 What was the Great Famine?

For an interactive overview of Famine experiences children could visit the following website:
http://www.irishpotatofamine.org/

Pages 6–7 Ireland before the Famine

Children could research the chronology of the Plantations in Ireland from the early Norman invasions to the Plantation of Ulster. They could create a timeline to include important events and a map showing areas planted by settlers during the various waves of settlement.

Oliver Cromwell's campaign in Ireland caused devastation all over the country. Children could research the various battles that were fought, the numbers of people who died and the effects of the campaign on the people of Ireland.

Pages 8–9 Potato blight

Children could do a simple maths task to work out how many potatoes it would take to feed a family of four for a certain period of time. The maximum amounts eaten per day were 60 for men, 45 for women and 30 for children.

Sir Walter Raleigh is said to have brought the potato back from one of his voyages. The life of Raleigh and his connection to Ireland could be investigated by children. He had extensive lands near Youghal in Co. Cork and was mayor of that town for a time in the late-sixteenth century. Children should also be encouraged to separate what is known to be historical fact about Raleigh from stories that have grown up about his character, such as spreading his cloak for Elizabeth I – a story unlikely to be true.

Pages 10–11 The land system

Although the peasantry in many European countries in the nineteenth century was often extremely poor, the Irish peasant existed in a more unbalanced society than elsewhere. The practice of rack-renting (demanding an unreasonably high rent) discouraged investment into housing and land. Children could be asked to dramatise the lives of the inhabitants of the Irish countryside, from the various perspectives – from landlord to labourer. The Irish Primary School Curriculum, History Teacher Guidelines, 1999 provides a more detailed description of this method on pages 112–113.

Strokestown House and Famine Museum is a good example of an Irish landlord's residence, which could be visited in person or at: http://www.strokestownpark.ie/museum.html

Pages 12–13 Peel's Brimstone

As well as the Relief Commission, Robert Peel set up a Scientific Commission to search for a cure for the blight. Children could research who was involved in this commission and what it found.

In a classroom setting, the 'conscience-alley' approach could be used. One child could take on the role of Robert Peel as he decides on his course of action. Half the group could advise him to stick to his laissez-faire principles, while the other half could persuade him to attempt to ameliorate the worst effects of the famine he knows will strike.

Pages 14–15 1846 – the crop fails again

Using the evidence presented in the eyewitness primary sources included on this spread, children could paint a large-scale 'before and after' scene of the Irish countryside in the autumn of 1846. This could also include the fields and dwellings mentioned on pages 10–11.

Pages 16–17 The workhouse

Before the Famine the workhouses were often half full at most. When the Famine struck, people overcame their aversion to these institutions out of sheer necessity. Children could dramatise the scene where a family is segregated into the different quarters of the workhouse, and describe their working day in a 'Big Brother'-style diary room.

Pages 18–19 Eviction

Children should be encouraged to have empathy for an evicted family. This idea could be explored by asking children to imagine that they are being evicted. What three items of importance could they choose to bring with them, remembering that they must travel light? Comparisons could be made with homeless people today.

Pages 20–21 Black '47

The children's writer Marita Conlon McKenna in Chapter 7 of her book *Under the Hawthorn Tree* (O'Brien Press) provides an accessible description of a soup kitchen. Children could read this chapter on its own and discuss their impressions of it, or alternatively read the entire novel. This could provide further opportunities for creative writing and drama.

The Famine caused the outbreak of several diseases, including typhus, dysentery and cholera. Children could research these diseases and find out how they were spread. They could also investigate how they were eventually eradicated and controlled, not just in Ireland, but also in other parts of the world.

Pages 22–23 Famine stories

The Famine is frequently remembered in ballads and verse from the nineteenth century. Examples of ballads from the period are 'Skibbereen'

and 'The Famine Year' by Lady Wilde. They often reflect great anger and bitterness at the treatment of the peasantry. 'The Fields of Athenry' by Pete St John, although a modern composition, also makes reference to the Famine. Children could listen to a recording of this song and try to compose their own short ballad or lament.

Pages 24–25 Emigration and the 'Coffin Ships'

Children could be provided with a blank world map on which to plot the destinations of the Irish Famine emigrants. They could find out where the main ports were and show the main routes of the voyages taken.

A model of a Famine Ship could be constructed by children in groups. There are some references for what coffin ships looked like on: http://multitext.ucc.ie/viewgallery/335

Pages 26–27 Legacy of the Famine

The population data discussed on this spread could be used to create a simple trend graph.

After the Famine, farmers stopped relying on the harvest and began rearing cattle and sheep as well as growing crops. Children could research the changes in farming practices after the Famine.

Children could research the lives of famous people with Irish roots such as Kennedy and Henry Ford.

BOOKS AND WEBSITES

The following books are appropriate to children ages 9–12:
Marita Conlon-McKenna, *Under the Hawthorn Tree* (O'Brien Press, 1990)
Duncan Crosbie, *Life on a Famine Ship* (Gill & Macmillan, 2005)
P. Feirtear and G. Seekamp, *The Irish Famine* (Blackwater Press, 1999)
Laura Wilson, *How I Survived the Irish Famine* (Gill & Macmillan, 2000)

The following websites give more information about various aspects of the Great Famine and life for the Irish people during this period:

http://www.irishpotatofamine.org/
Offers an interactive tour of the villages, workhouses and schools in the Irish countryside during the Great Famine.

http://www.workhouses.org.uk
Contains information on the locations of workhouses across the UK, as well as information about what life was like for their inhabitants.

http://www.ireland-information.com/irishmusic/skibbereen.shtml
Contains the lyrics and music to the ballad 'Skibbereen'.

Index